**RAINBOW
STUDIES
INTERNATIONAL**

A Special Gift

Presented to

Virginia Burgess

From

The Crossroads Choir

On the Occasion of

Dedicated Service

Date

Nov 12 - 1999

Creating Colorful Treasures™

GIFTS OF HOPE™

Every Day Is A New Day!

Compiled by Billy & Janice Hughey

RAINBOW
STUDIES
INTERNATIONAL

Creating Colorful Treasures™

Gifts of Hope™

Blank Journal

from the "Gifts of Hope™" Series
Copyright © 1998 by Rainbow Studies, Inc.
All rights reserved.

Published by: Rainbow Studies International, P.O. Box 759, El Reno, OK 73036

Design Concept by Rainbow Studies International and Design Life Studio.

ISBN 0-933657-61-7

1 2 3 4 5 6 7 8 9 - 02 01 00 99 98
Rainbow Studies International, El Reno, Oklahoma 73036, U.S.A.

Printed in the United States of America

RAINBOW
STUDIES
INTERNATIONAL

COLOR CODE GUIDE

GOD	SALVATION
DISCIPLESHIP	FAMILY
LOVE	WITNESSING
FAITH	COMMANDMENTS
SIN	HISTORY
SATAN	PROPHECY

themes

for Quotes &
Scripture

God

The Father

The Son, Jesus Christ

The Holy Spirit

The Word of God

Savior

Lord

Messiah

I AM

Lamb of God

King of Kings

Alpha & Omega

Be still, and know that I am God.... Psalm 46:10 NIV

PEOPLE SEE GOD EVERY DAY.
THEY JUST DON'T RECOGNIZE HIM.

PEARL BAILEY

_____

_____

_____

_____

_____

_____

_____

_____

_____

_____

_____

_____

_____

_____

_____

_____

_____

_____

_____

_____

_____

_____

_____

_____

_____

_____

_____

_____

God often visits us,
but most of the time we are not at home.

French Proverb

God warms his hands at man's heart when he prays.
John Masefield

When you have nothing left but God, then for the first time
you become aware that God is enough.

Maude Royden

_____
_____
_____
_____
_____
_____
_____
_____
_____
_____
_____
_____
_____
_____
_____
_____
_____
_____
_____
_____
_____
_____
_____
_____
_____
_____
_____

If God be for us, who can be against us? Romans 8:31 KJV

God is spirit . . . . God is one.
God is light . . . . God is love.

John 4:24   Galatians 3:20   1 John 1:5   1 John 4:8 all NW

God is and all is well. John Greenleaf Whittier

THERE IS COMFORT IN THE FACT
THAT GOD CAN NEVER BE TAKEN BY SURPRISE.

GABELEIN

God Almighty does not throw dice.
Albert Einstein

God is patient because eternal.   St. Augustine

God is a circle whose center is everywhere
and whose circumference is nowhere.
Empedocles

I am the Alpha and the Omega, the First and the Last,
the Beginning and the End.

Revelation 22:13 NIV

Jesus! it is the name which moves the harps of heaven to melody . . .
a gathering up of the hallelujahs of eternity in five letters.

Charles Spurgeon

Then Jesus told her, "I am the Messiah!"

John 4:26 TLB

I am the bread of life . . . .
John 6:35 KJV

I am the good shepherd . . . . John 10:1 KJV

I am the way, the truth, and the life. . . .

John 14:6 KJV

_____

_____

_____

_____

_____

_____

_____

_____

_____

_____

_____

_____

_____

_____

_____

_____

_____

_____

_____

_____

_____

_____

_____

I am the light of the world . . . . John 8:12 KJV

themes

Discipleship

for Quotes &
Scripture

Obedience

Praise

Service

Worship

Wisdom

Works

Commitment

Fellowship

Follower

Spiritual Gifts

Fruit

Jesus called out to them, "Come, follow me! And I will make you fishermen for the souls of men!" At once they left their nets and went along with him.
Mark 1:17-18 TLB

_____

_____

_____

_____

_____

_____

_____

_____

_____

_____

_____

_____

_____

_____

_____

_____

_____

_____

_____

_____

_____

_____

_____

_____

_____

_____

_____

_____

And no one can be my disciple who does not carry his own cross and follow me.   Luke 14:27 TLB

Don't bother to give God instructions;
just report for duty.
Corrie ten Boom

_____
_____
_____
_____
_____
_____
_____
_____
_____
_____
_____
_____
_____
_____
_____
_____
_____
_____
_____
_____
_____
_____
_____
_____
_____
_____

You cannot stay where you are and go with God. Henry T. Blackaby

**The great thing in this world is not so much where we are,
but in what direction we are moving.**

Oliver Wendell Holmes, Sr.

Whoever serves me must follow me;
and where I am, my servant also will be.
My Father will honor the one who serves me.

John 12:26 NIV

*Two men please God — who serves Him with all his heart
because he knows Him; who seeks Him with all his heart
because he knows Him not.*

Nikita Panin

God hasn't called me to be successful.
He's called me to be faithful.

Mother Teresa

God made you as you are in order to use you as he planned.   S. C. McAuley

Christ is not valued at all
unless he is valued above all.

St. Augustine

_____
_____
_____
_____
_____
_____
_____
_____
_____
_____
_____
_____
_____
_____
_____
_____
_____
_____
_____
_____
_____
_____
_____
_____
_____
_____

No pain, no palm; no thorns, no throne; no gall, no glory; no cross, no crown.   William Penn

In this old world of give and take
there aren't many willing to give all it takes.

Anonymous

When the going gets tough, the tough get going.

Knute Rockne

If opportunity doesn't knock, build a door.   Milton Berle

What matters is not the size of the dog in the fight,
but the size of the fight in the dog.

Dwight D. Eisenhower

Success seems to be largely a matter of hanging on after others have let go.   William Feather

The man who wins may have been counted out several times,
but he didn't hear the referee.

H.E. Jansen

What we do during our working hours determines what we have;
what we do in our leisure hours determines what we are.

George Eastman

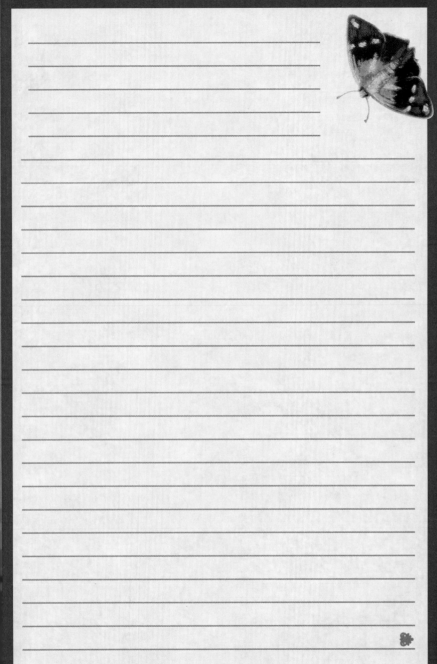

Making a living is important,
but living for the Maker is most important.
Janice Hughey

Common sense in an uncommon degree
is what the world calls wisdom.

Samuel Taylor Coleridge

To know the will of God is the highest of all wisdom.   Billy Graham

Wisdom is the quality that keeps you from getting
into situations where you need it.
Doug Larson

A man begins cutting his wisdom teeth the first time he bites off more than he can chew. Herb Caen

themes...

Love

for Quotes &
Scripture

Joy (Happiness)

Kindness

Mercy

Mourning

Lament

Comfort

Compassion

Peace

Sympathy

Humility

Charity

Love doesn't make the world go round.
Love is what makes the ride worthwhile.

Franklin P. Jones

_____

_____

_____

_____

_____

_____

_____

_____

_____

_____

_____

_____

_____

_____

_____

_____

_____

_____

_____

_____

_____

_____

_____

_____

It is better to have loved and lost, than not to love at all.   Alfred, Lord Tennyson

To love is to make of one's heart a swinging door.
Howard Thurman

Who, being loved, is poor? Oscar Wilde

The loneliest place in the world is the human heart when love is absent.

E. C. McKenzie

Love and a cough cannot be hid.

George Herbert

What the world really needs
is more love and less paperwork.
Pearl Bailey

Laughter is the shortest distance between two people.
Victor Borge

He who laughs, lasts! Mary Pettibone Poole

Laughter is a tranquilizer with no side effects.
Arnold H. Glasow

A laugh is a smile that bursts. Mary H. Waldrip

Enjoy the little things, for one day you may look back
and realize they were the big things.
Robert Brault

Most people are about as happy
as they make up their minds to be.

Abraham Lincoln

The bee is more honored than other animals,

not because she labors, but because she labors for others.

St. John Chrysostom

It's good sportsmanship to not pick up lost golf balls while they are still rolling. *Mark Twain*

It's not true that nice guys finish last.
Nice guys are winners before the game even starts.
Addison Walker

When things are bad, we take comfort in the thought
that they could always be worse. And when they are, we find hope
in the thought that things are so bad they have to get better.
Malcolm S. Forbes

*One reason a dog can be such a comfort when you're feeling blue
is that he doesn't try to find out why.*

Anonymous

Now I know I've got a heart, 'cause it's breaking.
The Tin Man (The Wizard of Oz)

_____
_____
_____
_____
_____
_____
_____
_____
_____
_____
_____
_____
_____
_____
_____
_____
_____
_____
_____
_____
_____
_____
_____
_____
_____

It is often hard to bear the tears that we ourselves have caused.   Marcel Proust

Believe me, every man has his secret sorrow, which the world knows not;
and oftentimes we call a man cold when he is only sad.
Henry Wadsworth Longfellow

_____
_____
_____
_____
_____
_____
_____
_____
_____
_____
_____
_____
_____
_____
_____
_____
_____
_____
_____
_____
_____
_____
_____

When I'm sad I sing, and then others can be sad with me. Mark Twain

Anyone can sympathize with the sufferings of a friend,
but it requires a very fine nature to sympathize with a friend's success.
Oscar Wilde

Rejoice with them that do rejoice, and weep with them that weep.

Romans 12:15 KJV

themes

for Quotes &
Scripture

Faith

Prayer

Miracles

Courage

Confession

Repentance

Fasting

Healing

Hope

Confidence

Conviction

Belief

When we do what we can, God will do what we can't. Anonymous

I tell you the truth, if you have faith as small as a mustard seed,
you can say to this mountain, "Move from here to there"
and it will move. Nothing will be impossible for you.
Matthew 17:20 NIV

Fear knocked at the door. Faith answered.
No one was there.

Anonymous

Faith is a refusal to panic.

D. Martyn Lloyd-Jones

Trust in God - but tie your camel tight.

Persian Proverb

Sorrow looks back, worry looks around, faith looks up.   Anonymous

Christians and camels receive their burdens kneeling.

Ambrose Bierce

_____

_____

_____

_____

_____

_____

_____

_____

_____

_____

_____

_____

_____

_____

_____

_____

_____

_____

_____

_____

_____

_____

_____

_____

_____

_____

_____

_____

_____

Any concern too small to be turned into a prayer is too small to be made into a burden. Corrie ten Boom

Do not pray for easy lives; pray to be stronger men! Do not pray
for tasks equal to your powers, pray for powers equal to your tasks....
Phillips Brooks

I have been driven many times to my knees
by the overwhelming conviction that I had nowhere else to go.
Abraham Lincoln

_____
_____
_____
_____
_____
_____
_____
_____
_____
_____
_____
_____
_____
_____
_____
_____
_____
_____
_____
_____
_____
_____
_____
_____
_____
_____
_____

_____
_____
_____
_____
_____
_____
_____
_____
_____
_____
_____
_____
_____
_____
_____
_____
_____
_____
_____
_____
_____
_____
_____
_____
_____
_____
_____

Courage is grace under pressure.   Ernest Hemingway

Have I not commanded you? Be strong and courageous.
Do not be terrified; do not be discouraged,
for the Lord your God will be with you wherever you go.
Joshua 1:9 NIV

Courage is resistance to fear, mastery of fear, not absence of fear. — Mark Twain

Courage is not the towering oak that sees storms come and go;
it is the fragile blossom that opens in the snow.
Alice Mackenzie Swaim

there's no substitute for guts.

paul "bear" bryant

Shoot for the moon. Even if you miss it
you will land among the stars.
Les Brown

A man who wants to lead the orchestra
must turn his back on the crowd.

Anonymous

_____
_____
_____
_____
_____
_____
_____
_____
_____
_____
_____
_____
_____
_____
_____
_____
_____
_____
_____
_____
_____
_____
_____
_____

I can do all things through Christ which strengtheneth me.   Philippians 4:13 KJV

My mother said to me, "If you become a soldier you'll be a general;

if you become a monk you'll end up as the pope."

Instead, I became a painter and wound up as Picasso.

Pablo Picasso

_____

_____

_____

_____

_____

_____

_____

_____

_____

_____

_____

_____

_____

_____

_____

_____

_____

_____

_____

_____

_____

_____

_____

_____

_____

_____

We are all worms, but I do believe I am a glowworm.   Winston Churchill

If you don't have confidence, you'll always find a way not to win.

Carl Lewis

Winning isn't everything,
but it beats anything that comes in second.

Paul "Bear" Bryant

_____
_____
_____
_____
_____
_____
_____
_____
_____
_____
_____
_____
_____
_____
_____
_____
_____
_____
_____
_____
_____
_____
_____
_____
_____
_____
_____

It's easy to make a buck. It's a lot tougher to make a difference.   Tom Brokaw

In matters of style, swim with the current;
in matters of principle, stand like a rock.

Thomas Jefferson

I make mistakes; I'll be the second to admit it. Jean Kerr

Right is right, even if everyone is against it,
and wrong is wrong, even if everyone is for it.
William Penn

We're all proud of making little mistakes.
It gives us the feeling we don't make any big ones.

Andrew A. Rooney

Many persons who appear to repent are like sailors
who throw their goods overboard in a storm, and wish for them again in a calm.
Mead

themes

for Quotes &
Scripture

Sin

Evil

Judgment of the Ungodly

Death

Hell

Curses

Condemnation

Temptation

Unbelief

Hatred

Hypocrisy

Apostasy

For all have sinned, and come short of the glory of God.

Romans 3:23 KJV

Sin is blatant mutiny against God. *Oswald Chambers*

Sin is not hurtful because it is forbidden,
but it is forbidden because it is hurtful.

Benjamin Franklin

While forbidden fruit is said to taste sweeter,
it usually spoils faster.

Abigail Van Buren

How immense appear to us the sins that we have not committed. Madame Necker

Sins are like circles in the water
when a stone is thrown into it; one produces another.
When anger was in Cain's heart, murder was not far off.
Philip Henry

The sin ye do by two and two ye must pay for one by one. — Rudyard Kipling

For God did not spare even the angels who sinned,
but threw them into hell, chained in gloomy caves and
darkness until the judgment day.
2 Peter 2:4 TLB

Better shun the bait than struggle in the snare.
John Dryden

But every man is tempted, when he is drawn away
of his own lust, and enticed.
James 1:14 *KJV*

Most people want to be delivered from temptation,
but would like to keep in touch.

Robert Orben

No degree of temptation justifies any degree of sin.   N. P. Willis

the TROUBLE WITH OPPORTUNITY IS THAT IT ONLY KNOCKS.
temptation kicks the door in.
anonymous

Few speed records are broken when people run from temptation. E.C. McKenzie

The only thing necessary for the triumph of evil
is for good men to do nothing.
Edmund Burke

WHEN YOU CHOOSE THE LESSER OF TWO EVILS,
ALWAYS REMEMBER THAT IT IS STILL AN EVIL.
MAX LERNER

There is a way that seems right to a man, but in the end it leads to death.   Proverbs 14:12 NIV

We go to the grave of a friend, saying, "A man is dead;"
but angels throng about him saying, "A man is born."
Henry Ward Beecher

Death is a camel that lies down at every door. Persian Proverb

Let us endeavor so to live that when we come to die
even the undertaker will be sorry.

Mark Twain

There are no atheists in the foxholes.

William Thomas Cummings

An atheist is a man who has no invisible means of support.

Fulton J. Sheen

Satan

False Teachers

Idolatry

Destruction of Idols

Demons

Devil

Serpent

Evil Spirits

False Prophets

False Worship

Witchcraft

Antichrist

Satan himself masquerades as an angel of light.

2 Corinthians 11:14 NIV

_____
_____
_____
_____
_____
_____
_____
_____
_____
_____
_____
_____
_____
_____
_____
_____
_____
_____
_____
_____
_____
_____
_____
_____
_____
_____
_____
_____
_____
_____

Satan was the first that practiced falsehood under saintly show.   John Milton

Satan is no fool; his timing is good;
he waits until you are in deep trouble,
and then he lets you have it.

Dale Evans Rogers

_____

_____

_____

_____

_____

_____

_____

_____

_____

_____

_____

_____

_____

_____

_____

_____

_____

_____

_____

_____

_____

_____

_____

_____

Jesus cut him short. "Be silent!" he told the demon. "Come out!"
The demon threw the man to the floor as the crowd watched,
and then left him without hurting him further.
Luke 4:35 TLB

The devil never seems so busy as where the saints are. Elizabeth Rundle Charles

Be sober, be vigilant; because your adversary the devil,
as a roaring lion, walketh about, seeking whom he may devour ....
1 Peter 5:8 KJV

The devil hath power to assume a pleasing shape.   William Shakespeare

It is not pleasant to believe that there is a personal devil,
but the question is not what is pleasant to believe
but what is true.
R.A. Torrey

Sin is like the little serpent aspis, which stings men,
whereby they fall into a pleasant sleep, and in that sleep die.
Swinnock

The snake stood up for evil in the Garden.

Robert Frost

Others try to worship things that are less than God;
it may be money, or ambition, or drugs, or sex.
In the end they find that they are worthless idols.

Desmond Tutu

Anything that comes between me and God is an idol — anything.... D.L. Moody

Be careful, or you will be enticed to turn away
and worship other gods and bow down to them.
Deuteronomy 11:16 NIV

_____
_____
_____
_____
_____
_____
_____
_____
_____
_____
_____
_____
_____
_____
_____
_____
_____
_____
_____
_____
_____
_____
_____
_____
_____
_____
_____

You can trust a crystal ball about as far as you can throw it.   Faith Popcorn

themes

for Quotes &
Scripture

Salvation

Blessings

Deliverance

Holiness

Heaven

The Tabernacle

Angels

Eternity

Resurrection

Second Coming

Judgment of the Godly

Grace

A man may go to heaven without health, without riches,
without honors, without learning, without friends,
but he can never go there without Christ.
John Dyer

There is salvation in no one else! Under all heaven there is no other name for men to call upon to save them.   Acts 4:12 TLB

❧

Morality may keep you out of jail,
but it takes the blood of Jesus Christ to keep you out of hell.
Charles Spurgeon

Carry the cross patiently, and with perfect submission; and in the end it shall carry you.

Thomas à Kempis

The cross is the only ladder high enough
to touch Heaven's threshold.

G.D. Boardman

There are no crownwearers in Heaven
that were not crossbearers here below.

Charles Spurgeon

Heaven is a prepared place for a prepared people.

D.L. Moody

So we fix our eyes not on what is seen,
but on what is unseen. For what is seen is temporary,
but what is unseen is eternal.
2 Corinthians 4:18 NIV

He who provides for this life, but takes no care for eternity, is wise for a moment, but a fool forever.   John Tillotson

the truest end of life is to know
the life that never ends.
william penn

WHERE WILL YOU BE SITTING IN ETERNITY? SMOKING OR NON? ANONYMOUS

The true saint is not one who has become convinced
that he himself is holy, but one who is overwhelmed
by the realization that God, and God alone, is holy.

Thomas Merton

The saints are the sinners who keep on going.
Robert Louis Stevenson

For fools rush in where angels fear to tread.   Alexander Pope

But men must know that in this theater of man's life
it is reserved only for God and angels to be lookers on.

Francis Bacon

Be not forgetful to entertain strangers: for thereby some have entertained angels unawares. Hebrews 13:2 KJV

The angel fetched Peter out of prison,
but it was prayer that fetched the angel.
Thomas Watson

When we let freedom ring, when we let it ring from every village and every hamlet, from every state and every city, we will be able to speed up that day when all of God's children, black men and white men, Jews and Gentiles,

Protestants and Catholics, will be able to join hands and sing
in the words of the old Negro spiritual, "Free at last! Free at last!
Thank God Almighty, we are free at last!"

Martin Luther King, Jr.

Reflect upon your present blessings, of which every man has many: not on your past misfortunes, of which all men have some.

Charles Dickens

_____
_____
_____
_____
_____
_____
_____
_____
_____
_____
_____
_____
_____
_____
_____
_____
_____
_____
_____
_____
_____
_____
_____
_____
_____
_____
_____
_____
_____
_____

Let me tell you that every misery I miss is a new blessing. Izaak Walton

Blessed is the person who is too busy to worry
in the daytime and too sleepy to worry at night.

Leo Aikman

Blessed are the flexible, for they shall not be bent out of shape.   Michael McGriff

themes

for Quotes &
Scripture

Family

Genealogies

Marriage

Sexual Concerns

Children

Parenthood

Home

Adultery

Fornication

Divorce

Friendships

Relationships

Where does the family start?
It starts with a young man falling in love with a girl.
No superior alternative has yet been found.

Winston Churchill

Therefore shall a man leave his father and his mother, and shall cleave unto his wife: and they shall be one flesh.   Genesis 2:24 KJV

The Christian is supposed to love his neighbor,
and since his wife is his nearest neighbor, she should be his deepest love.
Martin Luther

Marriage is like twirling a baton, turning handsprings,
or eating with chopsticks; it looks so easy till you try it. Helen Rowland

Even if marriages are made in heaven,
man has to be responsible for the maintenance.

James C. Dobson

Why does a woman work ten years to change a man's habits
and then complain that he's not the man she married?

Barbra Streisand

Before marriage, a man will lie awake all night thinking about something you said; after marriage, he'll fall asleep before you finish saying it.

Helen Rowland

Making the decision to have a child — it's momentous.
It is to decide forever to have your heart go walking around outside your body.

Elizabeth Stone

The greatest thing a father can do for his children is to love their mother. Josh McDowell

When you are a mother, you are never really alone in your thoughts.
A mother always has to think twice, once for herself and once for her child.

Sophia Loren

_____
_____
_____
_____
_____
_____
_____
_____
_____
_____
_____
_____
_____
_____
_____
_____
_____
_____
_____
_____
_____
_____
_____
_____
_____

Biology is the least of what makes someone a mother.   Oprah Winfrey

If you want your children to keep their feet on the ground,
put some responsibility on their shoulders.

Abigail Van Buren

_____

_____

_____

_____

_____

_____

_____

_____

_____

_____

_____

_____

_____

_____

_____

_____

_____

_____

_____

_____

_____

_____

_____

_____

_____

_____

_____

_____

Train up a child in the way he should go:
and when he is old, he will not depart from it.

Proverbs 22:6 KJV

In general my children refused to eat anything that hadn't danced on TV.   Erma Bombeck

Teen-agers were put on earth to keep adults from wasting time on the telephone.

Anonymous

When I was a kid, my parents moved a lot — but I always found them.   Rodney Dangerfield

Fatherhood is pretending the present
you love most is soap-on-a-rope.
Bill Cosby

Parents who wonder where the younger generation is going
should remember where it came from.
Sam Ewing

Nobody can do for little children what grandparents do.
Grandparents sort of sprinkle stardust
over the lives of little children.

Alex Haley

When you finally go back to your old hometown, you find
it wasn't the old home you missed but your childhood.

Sam Ewing

A man travels the world over in search of what he needs and returns home to find it.   George Moore

Where is home? Home is where the heart can laugh
without shyness. Home is where the heart's tears
can dry at their own pace.

Vernon G. Baker

It takes a heap o' livin' in a house t' make it home. Edgar A. Guest

Tact is the art of making guests feel at home
when that's really where you wish they were.

George E. Bergman

I have room for one more friend, and he is everyman.
Woody Guthrie

themes

Witnessing

*for Quotes &
Scripture*

Teaching

Counseling

Questioning

Instruction

Testimony

Ministry

Preaching

Evangelism

Gospel

Doctrine

Sayings

I look upon the world as my parish. John Wesley

Plead with the Lord of the harvest
to send out more laborers to help you,
for the harvest is so plentiful and the workers so few.
Luke 10:2 TLB

Lord, send me anywhere, only go with me.

Lay any burden on me, only sustain me.

Sever any tie but the tie that binds me to Thyself.

David Livingstone

You can't go on heavenly missions without heavenly fire.

D.L. Moody

My grand point in preaching is to break the hard heart,
and to heal the broken one.

John Newton

There is a net of love by which you can catch souls.   Mother Teresa

When you have a heart for God
you have a heart for ministry.
The two go hand in hand.
Jill Briscoe

_____
_____
_____
_____
_____
_____
_____
_____
_____
_____
_____
_____
_____
_____
_____
_____
_____
_____
_____
_____
_____
_____
_____
_____
_____

People want to know how much you care before they care how much you know. James T. Hind

I have found that I have no unusual endowments of intellect,
but I this day resolved that I would be an uncommon Christian.

David Livingstone

I am only an average man.
but I work harder at it than the average man.

Theodore Roosevelt

_____
_____
_____
_____
_____
_____
_____
_____
_____
_____
_____
_____
_____
_____
_____
_____
_____
_____
_____
_____
_____
_____
_____
_____
_____
_____
_____

The man who does not read good books
has no advantage over the man who can't read. Mark Twain

You ain't learnin' nothin' when you're talkin'.
Lyndon B. Johnson

_____
_____
_____
_____
_____
_____
_____
_____
_____
_____
_____
_____
_____
_____
_____
_____
_____
_____
_____
_____
_____
_____

If you want to get rid of somebody just tell 'em something for their own good.   Frank McKinney Hubbard

Talk low, talk slow, and don't say too much.

John Wayne

Plans fail for lack of counsel,
but with many advisers they succeed.

Proverbs 15:22 NIV

If it's free, it's advice; if you pay for it, it's counseling;
if you can use either one, it's a miracle.
Jack Adams

You see things; and you say, "Why?" But I dream things that never were; and I say, "Why not?"

George Bernard Shaw

Sometimes when we ask God our Why questions, instead of giving us answers he gives us himself . . . . Mary Jane Worden

_____
_____
_____
_____
_____
_____
_____
_____
_____
_____
_____
_____
_____
_____
_____
_____
_____
_____
_____
_____
_____
_____
_____
_____
_____
_____
_____
_____
_____
_____

There's nothing people like better than being asked
an easy question. For some reason, we're flattered
when a stranger asks us where Maple Street is
in our hometown and we can tell him.

Andrew A. Rooney

_____

_____

_____

_____

_____

_____

_____

_____

_____

_____

_____

_____

_____

_____

_____

_____

_____

_____

_____

_____

_____

_____

_____

Better to ask twice than to lose your way once.   Danish Proverb

Lead your life so you wouldn't be ashamed
to sell the family parrot to the town gossip.

Will Rogers

_____

_____

_____

_____

_____

_____

_____

_____

_____

_____

_____

_____

_____

_____

_____

_____

_____

_____

_____

_____

_____

_____

_____

WHEN YOU WERE BORN, YOU CRIED AND THE WORLD REJOICED.
LIVE YOUR LIFE IN SUCH A MANNER THAT WHEN YOU DIE
THE WORLD CRIES AND YOU REJOICE.
OLD INDIAN SAYING

Themes

for Quotes &
Scripture

Commandments

Offerings

Law

Priesthood

Feasts

Sabbath

Tithing

Baptism

The Lord's Supper

Church

Deacon

Growth

God's commandments are not just suggestions! Janice Hughey

And this is his commandment, That we should believe
on the name of his Son Jesus Christ,
and love one another, as he gave us commandment.
1 John 3:23 KJV

No man is above the law and no man is below it;
nor do we ask any man's permission
when we require him to obey it.
Theodore Roosevelt

PEOPLE OBEY THE LAW FOR ONE OF TWO REASONS:
THEY EITHER LOVE GOD OR FEAR PUNISHMENT.

JACK KEMP

The blood of the martyrs is the seed of the church.

St. Jerome

A church is God between four walls.   French Proverb

Don't stay away from church because there are so many hypocrites.

There's always room for one more.

Arthur R. Adams

_____

_____

_____

_____

_____

_____

_____

_____

_____

_____

_____

_____

_____

_____

_____

_____

_____

_____

_____

_____

_____

_____

_____

_____

The Church after all is not a club of saints; it is a hospital for sinners. George Craig Stewart

Let us not neglect our church meetings, as some people do,
but encourage and warn each other, especially now
that the day of his coming back again is drawing near.

Hebrews 10:25 TLB

Jesus spoke about the ox in the ditch on the Sabbath.
But if your ox gets in the ditch every Sabbath,
you should either get rid of the ox or fill up the ditch.

Billy Graham

themes

History

for Quotes &
Scripture

Creation

War

Times

Places

Journeys

Narration

Chronological
Record of Events

Vocations

Kings

Earth

Mankind

Christ is the great central fact in the world's history;
to him everything looks forward or backward.
All the lines of history converge upon him.
Charles Spurgeon

If all difficulties were known at the outset of a long journey,
most of us would never start out at all.

Dan Rather

Everyone journeys through character
as well as through time. The person one becomes
depends on the person one has been.
Dick Francis

Time is but the stream I go a-fishing in.
Henry David Thoreau

For the times they are a-changin'. Bob Dylan

Time and tide wait for no man.

Geoffrey Chaucer

_____
_____
_____
_____
_____
_____
_____
_____
_____
_____
_____
_____
_____
_____
_____
_____
_____
_____
_____
_____
_____
_____
_____
_____
_____
_____
_____

All my possessions for a moment of time.   Queen Elizabeth I (Last Words)

Any man's death diminishes me,
because I am involved in mankind;
and therefore never send to know
for whom the bell tolls; it tolls for thee.

John Donne

Every man's life is a fairy-tale
written by God's fingers.

Hans Christian Andersen

To save your world you asked this man to die;
Would this man, could he see you now, ask why?   W.H. Auden

You know you can be killed just as dead
in an unjustified war, as you can in one
protecting your own home.
Will Rogers

Mankind must put an end to war or war will put an end to mankind.   John F. Kennedy

There will be no veterans of World War III.
Walter Mondale

How hard it is to escape from places.
However carefully one goes they hold you –
you leave little bits of yourself fluttering on the fences –
little rags and shreds of your very life.
Katherine Mansfield

The place of crucifixion was near a grove of trees,
where there was a new tomb, never used before.
And so, because of the need for haste
before the Sabbath, and because the tomb
was close at hand, they laid him there.

John 19:41-42 TLB

People who make a living doing something
they don't enjoy wouldn't even be happy
with a one-day work week.

Edward "Duke" Ellington

Choose a job you love and you will never have to work a day in your life.   Confucius

Work spares us from three great evils:
boredom, vice, and need.

Voltaire

_____
_____
_____
_____
_____
_____
_____
_____
_____
_____
_____
_____
_____
_____
_____
_____
_____
_____
_____
_____
_____
_____
_____
_____
_____
_____

God gives every bird its food, but he does not throw it into the nest.   J.G. Holland

Prophecy

for Quotes &
Scripture

Promises

Covenants

Revelations

Vows

Visions

Dreams

Oaths

Pledges

Inspiration

Fulfillment

Future

Above all, you must understand that no prophecy of Scripture
came about by the prophet's own interpretation.
For prophecy never had its origin in the will of man, but men spoke
from God as they were carried along by the Holy Spirit.

2 Peter 1:20-21 NIV

_____
_____
_____
_____
_____
_____
_____
_____
_____
_____
_____
_____
_____
_____
_____
_____
_____
_____
_____
_____
_____
_____
_____
_____
_____

He that would know what shall be must consider what hath been.   Thomas Fuller

It is always wise to look ahead,
but difficult to look farther than you can see.
Winston Churchill

It isn't that they can't see the solution. It is that they can't see the problem. — G.K. Chesterton

When I look at the future
it's so bright it burns my eyes.
Oprah Winfrey

VISION WITHOUT WORK IS VISIONARY. WORK WITHOUT VISION IS MERCENARY.
VISION AND WORK TOGETHER, THEY ARE MISSIONARY.
ANONYMOUS

The very essence of leadership is that you have to have a vision.
You can't blow an uncertain trumpet.

Theodore Hesburgh

The poorest of all men is not the man without a cent;
it is the man without a dream.

Anonymous

We grow great by dreams. All big men are dreamers.   Woodrow Wilson

There are those who will say that the liberation of humanity,
the freedom of man and mind, is nothing but a dream.
They are right. It is the American dream.
Archibald MacLeish

_____
_____
_____
_____
_____
_____
_____
_____
_____
_____
_____
_____
_____
_____
_____
_____
_____
_____
_____
_____
_____
_____
_____
_____
_____
_____

Goals are dreams with deadlines. Diana Scharf Hunt

A rock pile ceases to be a rock pile
the moment a single man contemplates it,
bearing within him the image of a cathedral.

Antoine de Saint-Exupéry

_____

_____

_____

_____

_____

_____

_____

_____

_____

_____

_____

_____

_____

_____

_____

_____

_____

_____

_____

_____

_____

_____

_____

_____

_____

_____

_____

Two stonecutters were asked what they were doing.
The first said, "I'm cutting this stone into blocks."
The second replied, "I'm on a team that's building a cathedral."

Anonymous

The one who calls you is faithful and he will do it. 1 Thessalonians 5:24 NIV

I had rather do and not promise,
than promise and not do.

Arthur Warwick

Unclaimed promises are like uncashed cheques;
they will keep us from bankruptcy, but not from want.

Francis Ridley Havergal

Nothing is or can be accidental with God.

Henry Wadsworth Longfellow

You are more than a human being,
you are a human becoming.
Og Mandino

Memories are the key not to the past, but to the future.
Corrie ten Boom

No matter what a man's past may have been, his future is spotless.   John R. Rice

_____

_____

_____

_____

_____

_____

_____

_____

_____

_____

_____

_____

_____

_____

_____

_____

_____

_____

_____

_____

_____

_____

_____

_____

Anticipating is even more fun than recollecting.

Malcolm S. Forbes

_____
_____
_____
_____
_____
_____
_____
_____
_____
_____
_____
_____
_____
_____
_____
_____
_____
_____
_____
_____
_____
_____
_____
_____
_____
_____

The future ain't what it used to be. Lawrence "Yogi" Berra

Rainbow Studies International

ADDITIONAL PRODUCTS

❧ Other "Gifts of Hope ™" Series Selections

GIFT BOOK • Gifts of Love ™

GIFT BOOK • Gifts of Faith ™

GIFT BOOK • Gifts for the Family ™

GIFT BOOK • Gifts for Life's Journey ™

• Gifts of Hope Perpetual Calendar ™

The books in this beautiful series make wonderful gifts for special occasions or no occasion at all. Each book is in full-color with a focus on scripture, humor and heart-warming messages.

❧ A Rainbow of Hope ™ Gift Book

Throughout its 12 thematic chapters are 777 amusing and inspirational quotes, scripture verses and beautiful, original illustrations. Truly a "treasure book" for keeping or giving. Hardbound and gift-boxed.

❧ The Rainbow Study Bible ®

The most unique, yet useful study Bible in the marketplace today. Twelve colors represent twelve major themes throughout the entire Bible. Available translations include:

• New International Version • King James Version

• The Living Bible • Reina-Valera Revisión 1960 (Spanish)

• Portuguese